POETIC WORDSCAPES

Ranjana Rebelo Monteiro

First published in 2017 by

OpenCrayons.com
Wordit Content Design & Editing Services Pvt Ltd
Newbridge Business Centre, C38/39,
ParineeCrescenzo Building, G Block,
BandraKurla Complex, Bandra East,
Mumbai 400 051, India
T: 91 22 33040620

Copyright © 2017 by
All rights reserved. Any unauthorized reprint or use of this material is prohibited. No part of this book may be reproduced or transmitted in any form or by any means, electronic or mechanical, including photocopying, recording, or by any information storage and retrieval system without express written permission from the author/publisher.
Please do not participate in or encourage piracy of copyrighted materials in violation of the author's rights. Purchase only authorized editions.

©
ISBN 978-93-86487-06-3

Dedicated to my family

Acknowledgements

"But by the grace of God I am what I am, and His grace towards me has not been in vain. On the contrary I worked harder than any of them – though it was not I but the grace of God that is with me."

1 Corinthians 15:10

In writing this book I intend to thank the people who have influenced my life and helped me bring it to completion. The tireless and painstaking efforts of my parents have given me a head start in life and have raised me into the kind of individual that I am. My husband Joseph has rendered his support and encouragement while writing and publishing this book. My daughters Rhea and Raisa have patiently listened when I have read out my writings to them and have assisted me in editing the book besides giving their inputs.

My sincere gratitude to Sr. Caroline Duia FSP, Daughters of St Paul's for reviewing the contents of the book.

I would also like to thank all my friends who have been very much a part of my life and who have supported me through its ups and downs. I would have liked to mention their names here but the list would be endless. So cheers to you friends out there. Please know that in some way or the other you have contributed immensely to the writing of this book.

CONTENTS

SECTION I   PRAYER & WORSHIP

1.	Drooping Flowers	2
2.	The Radiance of the Dark	5
3.	The Eyes of my Heart	7
4.	Gazing at You	9
5.	To Be with You	11
6.	If I had not	13
7.	Lord, You Are Everything	16
8.	The Guiding Force of Faith	17
9.	A Confession of Wrongdoing	19
10.	Gifts from Above	20
11.	I Rely on You	21
12.	A Prayer of Thanksgiving	22
13.	The Reign of Divine Countenance	23
14.	Mercy Turned the Page	24
15.	My Hiding Place	26
16.	Guidance	28
17.	Your Gentle Touch	29
18.	God on My Side	30

POETIC WORDSCAPES

19.	The Lord's Faithfulness	31
20.	Faith : My Walking Stick	32
21.	The Recipe of Life	33
22.	Unity with God	34
23.	Justice Divine	36
24.	God's Love—The Only Constant	37
25.	In Faith, I Trust	38
26.	Ropes of Faith	39
27.	You Gave Me	41

SECTION II   SOCIETY & PEOPLE

1.	Listening is the Key	44
2.	The Authority of Words	45
3.	The Mall Culture	47
4.	The Old System	49
5.	If I Knew You	51
6.	In Need of Fellowship	53
7.	The Blessing of Friends	55
8.	To Live Alone	57
9.	Loneliness Haunts the Lonely	59
10.	You are Responsible	61
11.	There is Much Ahead	63
12.	Coach Dutifully	65

13.	True Justice	66
14.	Selfishness	68
15.	Worthiness of Life	69
16.	The World's a Place	71
17.	The Tale of Two Sides	73
18.	The Test of Obedience	75
19.	Unnecessary Suffering	76
20.	Money is No Healer	77
21.	Respect, Regard and Honor	78
22.	Power Analyzed	80
23.	In Hope of Divine Justice	82

SECTION III   FAMILY & EMOTIONS

1.	This Sacrament of Marriage	86
2.	Fruits of My Life	87
3.	Use and Abuse	88
4.	Parenting is an Art	90
5.	When the Family Fails	93
6.	God Guards His Children	97
7.	The Children's Play	98
8.	Raiding Fear	100
9.	Fear : The Ugly Monster	103
10.	Hello, Destiny?	105

11.	Oh, Dear! It's the Stress Again	107
12.	The Happiness Hunt	109

SECTION IV　　THOUGHTS OF LIFE

1.	Vice & Virtue	112
2.	Justice a Necessity	114
3.	Can't Have It All	115
4.	Chaos Unlimited	117
5.	Transient Living	119
6.	The Crossroads of Creativity	122
7.	To Cross a Stream	124
8.	Heaven and Hell	125
9.	The Margin of Error	128
10.	In Adversity's Face	129
11.	The Mode of Survival	131
12.	Black and White VS Wrong and Right	132
13.	Death in Sinking Sands	134
14.	The Wave of Pride	136
15.	The Essence of Spirituality	139
16.	The Stubborn Flowers	140
17.	The Time Accountant	142
18.	An Untraveled Path	144
19.	My Mission Carried Out	145

20.	The Eulogy of the Rejected Soul	147
21.	The Limit? What's That?	149
22.	Karma and Dharma	151

SECTION V   MELANGE

1.	Oneness with Nature	154
2.	The Stock Market in Verse	155
3.	The Aroma of Cooking	158
4.	The Flowers Tell...	159
5.	Operation Bug Evacuation	160
6.	A Lover's Fate	163
7.	The Poor Lad	166
8.	The Battle of the Bulge	168
9.	An Adventure	170
10.	The Pristine Peak	172
11.	The Rocket Experience	175
12.	A Ride in the sea	178
13.	Adjust your Sail	180
14.	Storm to Calm	182
15.	The Adventurous Artist	184
16.	To the Ends of the Earth	186
17.	All Good Things are Free	189

SECTION 1

PRAYER & WORSHIP

1

Drooping Flowers

Lord to pray and worship you,
I came to thy holy altar,
I bent my knee, I bowed my head,
I offered my sins, my falter.

There in front of you, lay a cut glass vase,
The most ordinary one I had ever seen,
In it were stalks of flowers and ferns,
They were far from colorful, bright and green.

They looked at me so pale, so weary,
Their petals wilted, edged with grey,
Some were shrivelled, their garments torn,
But still did their job and stood all day.

The better flowers were ornamental,
Sold to the rich at a great price,
The leftovers were cheaply discarded,
No one cared to look at them twice.

But you found them so valuable,
'Cause they're all part of what you made,
You cared to make them adorn your shelf,
Even though they were third grade.

Before they die and turn to dust,
You gave them a turn to sing your praise,
And to all who came to visit you,
Did their duty, they, their spirits did raise.

No great leader, no dignitary,
Had ever seen those drooping flower',
But to the broken, sick and weak,
They restored much strength and power.

Your awesome presence filled everything,
Their slight beauty and fragrance you did enhance,
From you they drew scented grace,
Your mercy, your kindness gave them a chance.

They've brightened up lives in plenty,
They were your tools divine,
They've soothed and so gently calmed,
Helped many escape the deep ravine.

That is how I am Lord,
Certainly not among the very best,
But this is all I have to offer you,
Allow me to serve you with all zest.

I will strive to give you pleasure,
My soul, my being will take no rest;
Your will, I cannot leave wanting,
Like those flowers even I'll pass heaven's test.

2

The Radiance of the Dark

When I see it, my heart skips a beat,
The feelings within are a delicious treat,
The sparkling glitter of the deed,
Oh! My heart within, how it does bleed.

But beyond the shine I see the sin,
The very same thing that'll land me in a bin,
So I call to God on high,
To come and help me when I sigh.

O Lord, My God I am weak,
You know that evil is at its peak,
I beg you, keep me from all wrong,
Send your Spirit and make me strong.

Lord, when temptation is steadily calling,
Prevent me from brutally falling,
Keep my heart, my mind pure,
Put a barrier and stop the lure.

POETIC WORDSCAPES

Lord, nail my desire on to a tree,
And let the pain set me free,
For thru' death to self I'll praise your name,
I'll glorify you in every game.

3

The Eyes of my Heart

God gave us the sense of sight,
To see the world he made,
Through it we can see his might,
And all imperfection begins to fade.

But not seldom we see so much wrong,
'Cause this very sense of sight,
Is blinded with so much pride,
And all we think is that only we are right.

Then we see in our neighbor's eye,
A speck that looks so large,
But how can the eye see within itself,
The log that is as big as a barge?

Did God fail to create for us?
A pair of eyes to look inward,
If he did, we would ourselves berate,
And move life's wheels forward.

Then we'll turn ourselves from out to in,
And changes within us make,
For only God's grace can make us win,
And vanity's roots in us shake.

4

Gazing at You

When I turn my gaze on you,
You change my focus, make it new.

Heartfelt sorrow, you turn to joy,
Tomorrow is made a colorful toy.

The doubt in me, you turn to faith,
I now walk through an open gate.

Fear is gone, I feel brave,
About your blessings, I shout and rave.

In my boredom, you show me a dream,
As delicious as white, smooth cream.

The insecurity has run away,
I feel secure in soft, brown hay.

Rejection and dejection have disappeared,
Love and acceptance have reappeared.

Heavenly rain has washed away pain,
Its gain, I get on the narrow lane.

It's gone the doom and the gloom,
My spirit, my soul goes Boom! Boom!

5

To Be with You

In front of you I love to sit,
And gaze at your lovely face,
Your charm, it fills my every bit,
I am engulfed in heavenly grace.

We set the time, the place and the date,
And you are always there,
But many a times, I skip, I'm late,
From afar at me you stare.

I always find some excuse,
To tell you why I couldn't come,
But you know it is just a ruse,
I try to solve my own life's sum.

Although I'd like to be with you,
To follow what you lay down,
I don't know why, my own will I pursue,
And avoid you like a clown.

Something forms an obstacle,
I know not what it is,
I cannot reach your pinnacle,
That is exactly what I miss.

To be one with you is what I want,
Through every moment of the day,
No barriers should ever daunt,
So I can with you stay.

6

If I had not

If I had not the wound in my heart,
I may never have sat at thy holy feet,
And if I was given a proper head start,
I may have been full of conceit.

If I had not the deep cuts in my flesh,
I may have never sought thy wondrous presence,
And if I was freed from my wire mesh,
I may have acted on my own and done nonsense.

If I had not been denied my prize,
You may have not found me before you kneeling,
And if I was allowed to bloom and rise,
In my own success I may have been with joy squealing.

If I had not been put through disgraceful shame,
Before you, you may have never found me prostrate,
And if I was given even a little fame,
I may have walked with pride, my head up and straight.

If I had never been thrown out and rejected,
Your Psalms and Word I may never have read,
But if my teachers in me, little hope projected,
I may have grown beautifully on your kingdom's bed.

If I was not cast away and humiliated,
My days in prayer I may have never spent,
But if those years of my life were satiated,
May be? Praises to your name I'd never vent.

But I am sure there was a kinder way,
For me to decide to follow you,
And definitely from your court I'd never stray,
Even if of heaven's riches I had my due.

For you've been harsh and very mean indeed,
As you have allowed me to suffer so much.
I'm sure you could have taken out every weed,
Even if your goodness, in humans, I could taste as such.

But I know that nobody wanted to like you act,
And be an image of you right here on earth.
They've acted against your holy will, that is a fact;
And so to wrongdoings and evil they have given birth.

But they did not know that it was between you and them,
They thought it was just them and me,
They acted without conscience or a guilty stem,
Let my suffering atone them, that's my plea.

7

Lord, You Are Everything

When I cry to you Lord, you always heed,
Waste no time to meet my need,
It is to you, Lord, that I pray,
I see the skies are dull and grey.

When life's burdens become too much,
It is you, who is my crutch,
With your help, I continue to walk,
And my lonely heart to you will talk.

You, O Lord are ever faithful,
Even though I am sometimes hateful,
When life's problems exasperate,
Lighten the load that I may recuperate.

Give me some time to revitalize,
And my potential fully realize,
You are my God, Holy Omnipotent,
You know all, Holy Omniscient

8

The Guiding Force of Faith

I put my whole trust in you,
And did exactly what I had to do,
Sometimes, I wonder if it was right,
Especially when my life was not very bright.

But what else could I have done?
All options ceased except this one!
Circumstances pointed to this way,
I had to keep other things at bay.

The constraints I had were choking me,
To find an optimum solution was the key!
You heard my supplications and my thanks,
You provided from your heavenly tanks.

So if all things don't seem to go very well,
I know that I will not land in hell,
I'll continue to beat my chest in prayer,
So you can't just stand and passively stare.

To my side you will come with haste,
And not a moment will you waste!
Though the blessings I cannot see,
I am convinced, you will be with me!

9
A Confession of Wrongdoing

I have done lots of wrong,
I've created a whole lot of stress,
Lord, you know that I'm not strong,
Please help me clear up the mess.

I have made many a mistake,
Some large, some big and some small,
Lord, let me not again them make,
Roll them out just like a ball.

On life's way I did blunder,
Though the wrongs may not be gross,
But in my ears they sound like thunder,
Put a shunt, drain out the dross.

I have learnt a lot from them,
Though the knowledge is full of pain,
On my life their scars have become a hem,
Closeness to you is my gain.

10

Gifts from Above

I thank you for all the splendid gifts,
That you on me bestow,
Their usage elevates and lifts,
Stimulates and keeps me in flow.

The fruits I get, I need to sift,
From pomp, selfishness and pride,
Or from you, I will drift,
On my own, I will begin to ride.

The prizes that the gifts did earn,
Should shine like jewels in your crown,
Their proper use is all I yearn,
Lest in your kingdom I should drown.

At your feet the gifts I lay,
Though not as good as myrrh or gold,
The path of the wise should be the way,
To worship you and your glory uphold.

11

I Rely on You

It is on you that I rely,
When uncertainties strike;
Your magnanimous power, I cannot deny,
I'll shout it from the roof top mic.

My anxious and my worried mind,
Was swirling round and round,
Peace and calm I tried to find,
But uneven and rough felt the ground.

I thought you had left and gone,
Leaving me alone in the lurch,
But it was faith that shone!
It led me to the nearby church.

Not gifts, but troubles! I laid before you,
And bowed my lowly head,
Petitions, intentions and many an issue,
Were the only words I said.

12

A Prayer of Thanksgiving

I am always very thankful,
For life's pleasures and its joys,
Forever I'll be grateful,
Whether I have new or broken toys.

Thru' all the ups and downs I've gone,
You've held me in your hand,
I could always feel your protecting brawn,
You've never dumped me in the sand.

Things could have gone from bad to worse,
If it was not for your grace,
I would've been without home or purse,
Hiding my shamed face.

There I go, to you I cling,
And in your great love I do bask,
My earthly life is just a fling,
But in it I've accomplished your task.

13

The Reign of Divine Countenance

You are my light, you are my source,
The only one who provides me resource.
On you I depend and on you I count,
Your faithfulness, I can only recount.
For the things you do for me, you do not charge,
But my diminishing energy you always recharge.
When complex life's matters I can't address,
You show me a way, get them to redress.
When intricate situations in front of me pose,
You provide me tranquility and a state of repose.
In my life Lord, many fires you did diffuse,
Whatever I ask of you, you never refuse.
I love you Lord, to me you are very dear,
I will always uphold you and you revere.

14

Mercy Turned the Page

In my room I sat and wept,
I was filled with anguish,
Remorse through my heart it swept,
Alone I began to languish.

With folded hands and many a tear,
I begged and with you pleaded,
That you would dissipate the cloud of fear,
Your comfort my spirit needed.

I asked for mercy and for pardon,
That through your love you, me forgive,
Oh please! I said let your heart not harden,
Put me thru' the purifying sieve.

I took an oath that I would change,
If you wiped clean my slate.
You did it! You turned the page,
My life, I entrusted to your will's fate.

The new board you gave me was clean and white,
A second chance again to start,
Beautiful designs you now could sight,
From your presence I will not part!

Intricately and finely I did inscribe,
My faith, my character I put to toil,
I would never dare to ever bribe,
This new white sheet I wouldn't spoil.

From the filth you me did lift,
As new life to me you gave,
To you I present it as a gift,
I promise to keep it from the grave.

You told me, to take life in my stride,
And not to get so tense,
This life on earth is but a ride,
Just act with common sense!

15

My Hiding Place

You are my hiding place,
It is in you that I hide my face.

A face, that's terror stricken,
That pales from dusky to ashen.

A face, that needs compassion,
To be freed from worldly passion.

A face, that is ashamed,
Of sins that cause it to be defamed.

A face, that's lost its glaze,
And which is in an enigmatic daze.

A face, that's completely lost,
It knows not how to pay the cost.

A face, that's turned and tossed,
When it is totally bossed.

But most of all; a face that has no place,
In this world's ruthless race!

16

Guidance

Lord, for guidance I turn to thee,
May your countenance fall on me,
In the pitch darkness I cannot see,
I pray humbly on a bended knee.

Lord, lead me on, don't let me be,
I don't want to encounter the stormy sea,
I can turn to you as I am free,
I pray humbly on a bended knee.

Lord, show me, from me don't flee,
This is my constant plea,
To do right and be your source and glee,
I pray humbly on a bended knee.

17

Your Gentle Touch

I am lonely, I am weak,
There is no one else but you to seek,
At your feet I sit so bleak,
As I wait for your gentle touch.

You're so strong, you are made of teak,
In this world I'm just a freak,
At your door I scratch and creak,
As I wait for your gentle touch.

In your presence I reach my peak,
And tears stop rolling down my cheek,
At my life please take a peek,
Thank you for your gentle touch.

18

God on My Side

I have got God on my side,
By his Word, it is I who will abide,
He supports me through every thick and thin,
He gives me strength to combat all sin.

God lives in me and I live in him,
He prunes my heart, he keeps it trim,
For in it he takes much delight,
I want to reform and do the right.

God my stance will vindicate,
If from wrongdoing I abdicate,
After cleansing me to the core,
Justice he'll bring to the fore.

One thing in my life I desire,
That the Lord's pleasure my actions will hire,
I am concerned only with how I behave,
As I want to avoid the living grave.

19

The Lord's Faithfulness

The Lord always answers me when I call,
For he loves me and he will never let me fall.
He builds me, he guides me and he me does safe-guard,
He ensures that my life is not very hard.

Difficulties and trials I do come across,
Those refine me and strain out the dross,
But in my heart I feel no angst or fear,
'Cause I know that he is always close and near.

I hear his Word, I do his will,
With peace my heart he always does fill,
When the fruits of my effort I lay at his feet,
My spirit is uplifted, contentment I meet.

20

Faith: My Walking Stick

I relied on faith to carry me through,
It has been rigorous, my skin's turned blue,
Weary have I been climbing the steep slope,
Prayer and surrender have been my dope.

It's been rough as I've had to trust,
At times my sustenance has been stale crust.
It has been hard to obey the voice of intuition,
For God and me, it is the conjunction.

I hope and hope and never give up,
No matter the type of broth in the cup.
Sometimes I cannot drink though it's an elixir,
But I swallow quietly, I down the mixture.

I know that at the end of the tunnel there is light,
Since it is dark, it I cannot sight.
Faith tells me, "Your in the palm of my hand,
I will carry you over sinking sand."

21

The Recipe of Life

The Lord gives and the Lord takes,
But my overall life, it is he who makes.
I wonder why he takes what he gives,
My life has to pass through many sieves.

He's constantly sieving my life's content,
And shaking me to a great extent.
One reason could be to distill out tar,
The other could be to aerate the flour.

Whatever the reason he wants the result,
That the cake bakes well and he can exult.
He wants it well risen, rich and light,
The creamy texture should enthrall those who bite.

For Lord you are the baker and I am the dough,
Lessen the rigors on the sieving floor,
Have mercy on me as I have less strength,
Simplify my test, reduce the length.

22

Unity with God

With God I can only unite,
When with my neighbor I do not fight,
For if with the latter I have fought,
Peace with God cannot be bought.

For in my neighbor lives the Lord,
We have to co-exist in one accord.
It is only then God I'll experience,
With my fellow beings I'll eliminate grievance.

To live in the Lord, is to with people unite,
Then brotherhood and holiness you will sight.
Humanity is more than just the essence of God,
It is God himself who lives in every human pod.

So if you want to know who he really is,
Be humane to all, make it your biz.
Little you may be bruised or slightly bashed,
But I assure you, you will never be smashed.

For the Lord supports all who live for him,
His responses are known just not a whim.
He will sustain and encourage you through,
Don't get disheartened, on the path there are few.

23

Justice Divine

Justice you have given, for justice I can see,
Justice my hope it livens, giving me hope to live free,
For you have kept your promise,
Vindicated my actions and my stance,
Reiterated that it's worth being good,
As you'll use it, to my life enhance.

You have upheld me with your hands,
And sorrowed with me my lost cause,
In faith I only had to wait for long,
As you appeared to sleep and pause.
But in your time, you've brought about
Justice, in front of one and all,
Judged in favor of my case,
You made sure that I didn't fall.

24

God's Love—The Only Constant

Know that God's love is ever constant,
It is always there to shelter you.
No matter what you are yourself,
Please avail your rightful due.

For if you encounter God's forgiving love,
Living your dharma will be without measure,
Karmic points you'll gain with ease,
The living experience will be a pleasure.

So use love's force that comes vertically down,
To fuel your life and guide your action,
You must create a successful paradigm,
In which you'll find God in action.

25

In Faith, I Trust

I've seen your face Lord,
I've heard your gentle voice,
And though the journey's rough,
I follow you by choice.

On my shoulders I bravely carry,
A cross that is so very heavy,
As I know any other way,
On me will impose a costlier levy.

My vision is blurred,
I cannot see far,
My speech is broken and slurred,
And life, at times has been a little sour.

Lord, in you alone, I put my faith,
You are my refuge, for you I'll patiently wait.

26

Ropes of Faith

When I find it hard to you pray,
And my voice sounds like a donkey's bray,
I try to focus and concentrate on you,
But I can't for my problems are far from few.

Then I just rely on the gift of faith,
Knowing that you've never forsaken me till date,
I find myself just drifting by,
With no end in sight I cannot even cry.

In those times my Lord, I can't feel you there,
I try to find you and search everywhere,
But from the past, I know you are closest to me,
And you'll carry me high, through it, me you'll see.

I love you Lord, you are my only hope,
Please help me enact my role in life's soap,
O my Lord, I cannot even mouth a prayer,
And helpless at your loving face I stare.

POETIC WORDSCAPES

Distraught my Lord, in front of you I sit,
Life has beaten me hard and I've been hit,
In these moments of pain I'm distressed,
Down and out and for resources hard-pressed.

I just remind myself that you give to one and all,
And to my aid you'll come even before I call,
For you have always been my fortress and my strength,
To save me Lord I know you'll go any length.

I thank you Lord for the faith that on me you bestow,
It is by this rope, you, me to calmness tow,
In the midst of gutsy wind and stormy sea,
Your reputation is to take control and protect me.

27

You Gave Me

When I was discarded by each and every one,
You were the one who held me close,
And you whispered in my ears, "You're worth a ton."

When I spoke and there was no one to hear,
You were the one who empathized with me,
And muttered, "My child take courage, do not fear."

When all were to me unfair and unjust,
You held my hand, upheld my cause,
And said, "Take this free gift of faith and trust."

When I was hounded and I had to flee,
You took my place and stood my ground,
And in front of all, you put forth my humble plea.

When I was distraught and completely worn,
You gave my heavy head a bed to rest,
And with your holy hand you sewed my spirit torn.

When I was worried and full of stress,
You gave me hope to sort out the mess,
And put a song of praise upon my lip,
Allowed me, to from your bounty sip.

Section II

Society & People

1

Listening is the Key

Many times I fail to listen,
To discomfort and pain,
I try to cover all with glisten,
Fool myself and say that all is gain.

The voice that is lost has to speak,
In uglier ways it does shout,
The pain has now made the other weak,
There is no way to turn about.

In deadly disease it gets expressed,
And with sorrow the victim cringes,
For most sickness is pain suppressed,
On love and kindness the victim binges.

By then it might be very late,
For consequences have already been borne,
But Lord with a miracle open life's gate,
So those who suffer are not torn.

2

The Authority of Words

The words I speak,
They have much power,
To cure and heal,
To steer the wheel,
To be a soothing balm,
Or cast a gentle calm.

The words I speak,
Can be a shower,
To rain down blessings,
On all God's nestlings,
To give his grace,
To every weary face.

The words I speak,
They can be many a flower,
To brighten the life,
Of someone in strife,
To give food to the starving,
In their hearts, a niche carving.

POETIC WORDSCAPES

The words I speak,
Are like a tall tower,
They set more than one rule,
Make one wise or a mule,
Can build and construct,
Or break and destruct.

The words I speak,
Should remind me of a sower,
With temperance to be spoken,
To give wisdom as a token,
This is all that I seek,
That my neighbor becomes strong, not weak.

3

The Mall Culture

I entered the bright and sprawling hall,
It was the lobby of the magnificent mall.

Like mushrooms everywhere they have sprouted,
Displaced the old and culture routed.

They have brought much into the city,
Given it a face-lift and made it pretty.

Entertainment, games and fun,
Teens and youngsters are on the run.

The children play in the kiddie's zone,
With doll house, toy car and telephone.

The others find their joy in shopping,
With bags full their shoulders are dropping.

Food courts, coffee bars and parlors of ice-cream,
Wow! The appetites within people scream.

To gorge on all that is available,
You need to think, is it affordable?

Global goods have been brought to our door,
Desi ground is now an international floor.

Spending and credit is on the increase,
Individual saving has seen a decrease.

The income gap between rich and poor is glaring,
You come out and see beggars staring.

The rich find these malls a material haven,
The poor see social justice unshaven.

The mall experience is here to stay,
For those who have money cheques to pay.

4

The Old System

A system was formulated to exist,
It was drawn by men of ancient,
Its objective was to govern and assist,
Towards order they had a penchant.

The system was used for years and years,
But after much time it became outdated,
It satiated needs and abolished community fears,
But soon a new one had to be stated.

The old system served to provide and navigate,
But time could not stop itself from unfolding,
Though the system had no scope to accommodate,
On societal transformation it had a holding.

The system which once received much applaud,
For being swiftly efficient and effective,
Was now to the youngsters a scammer and a fraud,
They were convinced not to make it their elective.

The young could never fight the system,
As the elders dominated and suppressed,
Obedience was the bate, the virtuous stem,
By which the young were coaxed to not feel oppressed.

So fighting against time they tried to abide,
But with sorrow their spirits were tolled.
The pitch was dark and rough but they had to tide,
Silently they sacrificed and they were bowled.

5

If I Knew You

If I knew you and you knew me,
Then eye to eye we would see,
There'd be no ground for us to disagree,
Of strain and stress we'd be free.

If we could discuss what's on our mind,
And a common platform we could find,
Then the sinuous coil we could unwind,
We'd see deep friendship trailing behind.

If we could speak in an explicit manner,
Then all matters implicit would be under the hammer,
There would be no reason to dishonestly stammer,
Our speech would be eloquent with perfect grammar.

So every encounter that I have with you,
Should strive to drive away the dreary blue,
I should get to know you as a person,
Improve our relations and stop it from worsen'.

POETIC WORDSCAPES

I could do that if I could with you abide,
And examine our thoughts side by side,
Lies we shouldn't tell and truth we shouldn't hide,
In nearness and togetherness we'd make a big stride.

6

In Need of Fellowship

I asked many questions and advice I much took,
For there was no available, ready reckoning book,
With no established rules as to what to do,
I had to find out from many and from few.

Opinions they gave and paths they chartered,
Confused I got with the knowledge I carted,
All parameters, fixed and variable I analyzed,
But a decision I couldn't arrive at, I was paralyzed.

Finally I sat still and began to discern,
The vast array of probability and concern,
I zeroed in on an entailing alternative,
But I couldn't take the final step, I froze contemplative.

I had to be pushed, counseled and coaxed,
Fellowship I needed, I couldn't live without folk,
For the company of people is of arrant importance to me,
It helps my mind decide and makes my eyes see.

7

The Blessing of Friends

Some friends are to laugh, some friends are to play,
Some are very serious and some are quite gay,
Some friends console me and some friends prod me on,
Some are very encouraging while some have temporarily gone.

Some friends listen to me, some friends give advice,
Some are very supporting and others are like spice,
They are all so different as characters are diverse,
But they all form a vital part of my universe.

Each one is so unique, an essential part of a jigsaw,
None can be lost as the puzzle will then have a flaw.
For all have a role in my life to play,
And they form the Vitamin F pill that strengthens me each day.

My friends for me are an invaluable treasure,
As they contribute to my happiness in full measure,
The pleasure of friends decreases my stress,
As my burdens they definitely make much less.

I pray to God to all of them bless,
And increase them in number, I'll pay the extra cess.

8

To Live Alone

So close and yet so far, unity is a distant star,
A star so far, just a dot of twinkling light,
Eye strain is necessary for one to sight.
Like mindedness is absent, it cannot be got,
Oneness eludes because of distorted thought.

Egos are huge they clash all the time,
To the tune of selfishness their lives chime.
Self-exultation is their song and their rhyme,
And to execute it they've acquired the required skill;
Plans are chalked out rejecting God's will.

Tolerance is non-existent and so is goodwill,
Loving acceptance of each other does not fit the bill,
Each one for himself and none for all,
One will have to cope by one's self even if there's a fall,
As each is an alien with no common ground to be found.

So in the end we have persons fiercely independent,
Each lives in a cubby hole lonely and despondent,
That on them has taken a toll, as inter dependence was never a goal.
Of God in each other they've got no experience,
And that is the main and sole grievance.

Alone they live and alone they sigh,
And when the end comes alone they die,
But just before death all relations they want to make straight,
As they think they'll get free passes into heaven's gate.
They may get it but they have lost out on life!

Realize one and all, you can't be an unsociable cuss,
Compromise and give in without making a fuss.
Divine grace will aid all those who for unity stand,
It will lead you and guide you by holding your hand.
Take it, don't leave it, in God you must trust!

9

Loneliness Haunts the Lonely

Loneliness, yes, it is a disease,
An illness, it is of the human soul,
When nobody wants to meet you and talk,
On life's path you'll tread sole.

Loneliness of it, are you the cause?
Did your temperament lead others away?
Introspection of self, you may have to do,
Or you will find yourself left alone by the way.

On Almighty God who is in heaven,
Day and night you must meditate,
So that his love you'll feel all around,
And in your life he'll mediate.

POETIC WORDSCAPES

Your relationship with God needs to improve,
And also what you think of self,
Then with others automatically you'll bridge all feuds,
Unlike a wallflower you won't be left on the shelf.

10

You are Responsible

Be careful my friends, hear what I say,
Indignation don't create, on you, it will fall one day,
A downpour it will be, and it will be non-stop,
You'll be crying for mercy from your house-top.

For although, God loves you with all his might,
His hands will be tied and the knots will be tight,
For your bad behavior my friends, has created wrath,
With your stubbornness, it is a consequence that you have bought.

For God has warned you on many occasions in the past,
You did not pay heed, you turned away fast.
In love, he sent his angels to make you understand,
But you took him for granted; played your own band.

So what can be done, if you did not listen,
You committed sin to make your own life glisten,
He wanted to help you but you cast him behind,
And now it is difficult for you, God to find.

For God does not show his wrath, you on yourself
it bring,
And through your wickedness, curses you in ring,
For fury and scourge, on yourself you've brought,
The consequences are yours to bear in both
hardship and drought.

11

There is Much Ahead

Friend, don't give up, it's not the end,
Just look up a little, there's much round the bend,
Much of better and certainly not of worse,
Your life my dear, is not a curse.

The ravine you are in, may be a living hell,
You crashed in it and hard you fell,
But there's someone who loves you very much,
And as you read these words your heart, he'll touch.

My friend, he'll lift you up from the deep,
Just extend your hand; his angel will help you leap,
You'll leap to a height you've never known,
To experience God's goodness, you must be prone.

So much you have learnt from this hard bang,
Let it not go waste, help your buddy in pang,
That's how you will be God's angel to him,
Together you'll worship the Almighty with a sacred hymn.

12

Coach Dutifully

You have to coach, you have to train,
But you have to do it in love, that's the only reign,
If you are a teacher, parent or boss,
Ensure that your subordinates don't go for a toss.

Coach your ward in an unselfish manner,
Right teaching should be the rule of the banner,
Keep in mind the good of all in concern,
Guaranteed respect will be your return.

Faithfulness and loyalty to you will only grow,
Honor and obedience to you will just flow,
Motivated will be all under your care,
Laziness and sloth will be very rare.

Do the above and you won't go wrong,
To get peace overall it won't be long,
Happiness and calm will be the name of the game,
The reason to live won't be lame.

13

True Justice

It is true justice that is a victim's desire,
Revive the cinders, set ablaze the fire,
Let it burn up all untruths and lies,
Let it give heed to innocent cries.

For it is with the sceptre that God does rule,
And no one can ever him, try to fool,
He knows the truth; he won't let you down,
He'll speak with authority, wearing a holy crown.

The victim's been wronged and mutilated,
Wrenched to the bone and humiliated,
In a cunning way the victim's been banished,
Thru' dubious methods, his name has been tarnished.

No place to cry, no one to tell,
No one to listen, the wrongdoer does hard sell.
God has seen the victim cast in a deep well,
He unites with the soul and in the victim he does dwell.

He'll fight on behalf of those who lack spirit,
He'll stand guard to the soul of the maligned ferret,
No matter how much the wrongdoer tries to him dodge,
He'll uncover the past, he won't allow forge.

For the innocent, they cannot take revenge,
The poor will never be able the rich avenge.
It is God who will bring about the required circumstance,
The wrongdoer will kneel with repentance.

14

Selfishness

You people have no graciousness,
You people have no manners,
You are devoid of all nobleness,
Selfishness is the base of all your banners.

Only of self you do think,
In society this raises a stink,
In this way you yourself isolate,
Because all social norms you violate.

But actually this is foolishness,
That takes the form of stark selfishness,
For in the end, it is you, who'll suffer,
You've allowed it to rule your life, you duffer!

15

Worthiness of Life

Be careful my friends when you sin,
'Cause sin causes much sufferin',
May be of self you have no esteem,
Or, may be, you have a selfish dream.

Does your self-esteem run very low?
Then take someone's help, who your life can tow,
And if you have a big, fat, selfish dream,
Then don't be sour like spoilt cream.

For your nastiness to self or to neighbor,
Will in the end destroy the fruits of your labor,
Be kind and gentle with yourself,
And do the same with everyone else.

For everyone's holy and precious to God,
All conglomerate together with his sacred cod,
Let all human knots weave a carpet with a good design,
And hand it over for future generations to sign.

POETIC WORDSCAPES

It will be a carpet which is rich in beauty,
And it will bring comfort to all, inform them of their duty.

16

The World's a Place

The world is a large playing field,
Where things are right and wrong,
The Lord helps us to correctly yield,
Keeps us safe and makes us strong.

Trust and faith is the shield,
When we walk through its tempting lure,
Thy Word is the sword we wield,
That keeps us clean and pure.

Protect us from the burning arrow,
Let it our beings not pierce,
For worthy living on every morrow,
May our battles not be fierce?

Let us not from you stray,
When bad friends and peers us coax,
Guide us back, show us the way,
Make us realize the hoax.

To live in this world and yet apart,
Requires God's courage, strength and grit,
But that is our calling from the start,
Or many problems we will knit.

It is difficult to be different from the rest,
For friends and peers are priceless,
Let us not act on false behest,
Make us uncanny, not foolishly mindless.

Help us Lord to worship thee,
And not the world around,
As we genuflect on bended knee,
The right balance in our ears sound.

We have a calling and a mission,
That's why we are born on earth,
Through us, you create a cosmic fusion,
And of your love there is no dearth.

17

The Tale of Two Sides

"It is in giving; that we all do receive",
That is what we are taught to believe,
With this truth, a new nature we must conceive,
A different attitude we must perceive.

For giving is just one-half of the truth,
To make it a reality selflessness is the route,
We must not act like a hardened brute,
Counting the cost and expectation shouldn't take root.

To receive and accept is the other part,
To take with humility it hurts the heart,
For if we cannot receive, we cannot start,
Our stupidity will upset the apple cart.

Beware! It is not the age-old system of barter,
Exchange is not the rule of the charter,
We may have to give to someone without taking back,
Receive from still another without rendering a sack.

In this way someone will know God's love,
And in this way we will receive God's abundant love,
The experience of his infinite power is all encompassing,
And the fire of his love is all consuming.

18

The Test of Obedience

To obey is a sacrifice,
'Cause you put yourself at stake,
At times you will freeze like ice,
When authority does demand and take.

To obey is more than an offering,
In money or in kind,
For it is your own will suppressing,
It puts your desires behind.

To obey causes stress to heighten,
To the eyes brings a whole lot of tears,
Yet character it does strengthen,
In all life's varied spheres.

To obey can mold and make you,
And discipline inculcate,
It is the test and it does hew,
Your personality it will cultivate.

19

Unnecessary Suffering

Unnecessary suffering is all around,
'Cause humans lack what is grace,
In our behavior, thoughts and deeds,
Social norms and barriers delineate like lace.

To our pride and ego we are steadfast,
Resist and guard against all change,
Refuse to move an inch or less,
As we watch our dearest singe on the range.

The onus lies on the older and the stronger,
To adapt and accept the new,
For the younger are inexperienced,
They just know that life is calling you.

God's ways are many and diverse,
Our limited minds cannot understand,
But with openness yield to them,
So life gets flavor and is not bland.

20

Money is no Healer

A victim's compensation cannot be money,
For it cannot act like soothing honey,
No amount of it can sweeten,
A soul that is smothered and brutally beaten.

Money is not the solution,
For it cannot cause dilution,
Of feelings caused by rejection,
Or grave and inhuman humiliation.

Money, an elixir, it cannot be,
Even when poured out like a sea,
It is love and respect which is the need,
Only with it a bruised soul can be freed.

That takes time and painstaking effort,
If it really has to bring comfort,
An outpouring of money can be the quick cure,
But healing it cannot bring for sure.

21

Respect, Regard and Honor

Respect, regard and honor,
Are three things we'd all like to get,
But they don't come so very easily,
That premise we must not forget.

To get them one cannot order,
As they must all be earned,
For ordering and bullying is immature,
That fact must be learned.

Authority cannot be forced,
As the opposite it will bring,
For there may be times you appear to succeed,
But your talk will be the despised thing.

To earn them it takes lots of effort,
That does not go in vain,
Pride, you'll have to swallow,
And that will be the real pain.

However that pain is worth it,
For it is a corollary of the choice to love,
But the torture of disrespect, disregard and dishonor,
Is a result of the choice that is all but love.

Your intention may be very noble,
May be to discipline and perfect,
But if it is done without a healthy love,
Only hate and ill feeling it will effect.

So my friend I adjure,
To sacrifice some part of yourself,
So that in love we may always live,
And strong bonding we don't shelf.

22

Power Analyzed

A powerful position for it, if you aspire,
The seat is transient; it is only on hire,
Today it comes with pomp and glory,
Tomorrow you may be the protagonist of a tragic story.

If that place for you was retained,
Then till the end, in it you'll be sustained,
But if it is not, don't it seek,
Or you'll find yourself slipping from the peak.

Power may be false and it can corrupt,
Your buried ego will grow to erupt,
You, it will seize and take total control,
You'll expect all to salute you when you stroll.

Another truth is that power can make you a puppet,
You'll find yourself singing the higher up's duet,
The boss plays a ventriloquist, you'll repeat his tune,
Your thoughts and opinion he'll influence and prune.

Responsible power will never make you someone's slave,
Misuse of it will never be done by the brave,
Many virtues and goodness from it will effuse,
Major battles and disagreements it will diffuse.

23

In Hope of Divine Justice

Too much has he suffered, too much has he slogged
Too much has he borne, his life, him has flogged,
With burdens so heavy, he walks in the hot sun,
With worries so many, there's no place to run.

There's no one to share, there's no one to trust,
He sits in the corner like an old burnt crust,
He hopes that Providence will have mercy on him,
And bring back joy to his face with a reassuring hymn.

Inexperienced has he been and innocent too,
That has in his heart, deep ridges hewed,
Without knowing, he has allowed others to in his field play,
And they have deposed him, for themselves to stay.

Now he is homeless with no one to care,
In a street shanty he sits with a despondent stare,
He hopes that God is just and will someday act,
Bringing truth to the fore and exposing every fact.

Section III

Family & Emotions

1

The Sacrament of Marriage

The Sacrament of Marriage, it is bliss,
A blessing from above, a divine kiss,
In this mystical union, we covenant with the Lord,
In harmony we live both in one accord.

The Sacrament of Marriage, it gives us grace,
It is more than a blessing to the human race,
With one's spouse one feels secure,
And more of the Lord's countenance, we can procure.

The Sacrament of Marriage, life it enhances,
To self and to couple it gives many chances,
To grow with each other and finally the Lord to reach,
Through it God's love we can feel and preach.

2

Fruits of My Life

My children are my priceless treasure,
The source of my utmost pleasure,
Their worth, no calibration scale can measure.

They are the mirror in which I see my reflection,
A part of my body, just an extension,
Their nearness brings my senses to elation.

In the children I find much truth,
Their words and their deeds bear much fruit,
In their lives, the future takes its root.

I am the vehicle that brought them this way,
They are mine to enjoy only today,
Responsibly, may I care for them is what I pray.

3

Use and Abuse

Children, Oh what are they?
They are born to laugh and play,
With their laughter and wondrous smiles,
They make us forget all our wiles.

Children, they are the product of love,
They are sent to us from above,
Their birth on earth is joyous news,
With their milestones, they us amuse.

Children, they're not meant for our personal use,
For that is nothing but large scale abuse,
If we do not listen to their cries and mews,
Their personalities will be subject to skews.

Children, they're God's gift to us,
It is difficult to raise them with all their fuss,
After painstaking efforts, we need to give back,
And in our parental duty we must not be slack.

If we keep them only for ourselves,
The child, in search of his inner self delves,
His life he will find pointless,
The despairing situation will be hopeless.

The child on you will then bring insult,
Whatever the matter he'll never you consult,
You will find yourself in a living grave,
And his love you'll begin to crave.

Even if the child does his best to honor you,
Love and respect will be absent that is true,
For you have exasperated him to the core,
His heart you've hurt and it is sore.

The child's life you will destroy,
Wicked deeds should not be used as a ploy,
They help nobody but bring disaster,
Oh Parent! Please don't be sinister!

Lord, I pray for all parents here and now,
That right parenting you may show them how,
So in the end, all will your name bless,
And life on earth will never be a mess!

4

Parenting is an Art

An artist who begins a painting,
Gets a new canvas white and clean,
Then with colors of different types,
He strives to get the required sheen.

The time taken is much more than minutes,
As painstakingly he gets the glow,
The effect of light and other nuances,
Keeps his creative energy in flow.

At times he works for days and months,
To finish the work that he did start,
For perfection is what he desires,
He won't rest till it satisfies his heart.

In the end his piece he exhibits,
And puts it in a gallery to display,
Where onlookers, it stimulates,
And re-energizes them to continue life's play.

The price it fetches, tells its value,
That's exactly what someone's mind will perceive,
For the price rests in its demand,
Its actual worth one really can't conceive.

The same is with a newborn's parents,
They're given a human canvas, white and clean,
On it they work with all their effort,
They strive to get required sheen.

The time taken seems just endless,
As painstakingly sleepless nights they spend,
Continuously they work to clean and feed,
Their work list never seems to end.

Eighteen years is what it takes,
For parents who strive to bring out the best.
Frustrating it may be at times,
But once they start, they cannot rest.

As childhood and teenage years do fade,
The adult into the world they send,
So that the person they have co-created,
Will for oneself and many others fend.

If the new personality can repair,
Mend broken bridges and build new,
To make the world a better place,
The parents have completed and done their due!

The difference between an artist and them,
Is that the former can midway the canvas, throw?
That option the latter does not really have,
As the child in some way will be developmentally slow.

So now you know how important it is,
For parents of every race and kind,
To take their duty very seriously,
Or peace and progress, the world will never find.

5

When the Family Fails

When the family fails, only on grace you can rely,
When close ties are not, and on no one's shoulder you can cry,
When they desert you, every moment you'll sigh,
And when your nearest reject you, you'll whine, "Why?"

A family has to support you each and every time,
They have to you love even if you commit a crime,
For it is love that unites, makes life sublime,
And if they don't, they'll be out of chime.

When the family disregards and discards,
Loving acceptance of you is not one of their cards,
Believe me, life for you will be very hard,
And you'll wait for God, to respond and be your guard.

In those hard circumstances, on grace if you call,
It will arise, hold you up, won't let you fall,
God will send angels as he hears your call,
He'll care for you and clothe you in love's shawl.

Family ties are something holy and divine,
They give you happiness; your face will shine,
For parental love is the closest to God's,
Unconditional in nature, it imitates the Lord's

But my friend, if that is sadly absent,
Then others will fool you through ways that are errant,
After being ragged, the Almighty you'll seek,
Rely on him my friends your life he'll tweak.

So when brothers and sisters, uncles and aunts,
God parents and cousins for you they can't,
Spare even a little time to listen to your cries,
No efforts they make to keep in touch or renew ties.

What's the use of all of them, you feel like an orphan,
They don't care two hoots, if you land in a coffin,
So make siblings and cousins of those who know the Lord's will,
And they'll make your life a heaven, the vacuum they'll fill.

But you all the relatives, please do realize,
That eventually blood ties, you can't ignore but recognize,
In its time you'll find, what I write is the very plain truth,
But then you'll be all alone, saying life hasn't borne fruit.

The time will be late; the hours won't be left,
Lonely in a rocking chair, you'll sit bereft,
Nobody will support you, nobody will care,
You've burnt all bridges, there's no chance to repair.

So be wise all who read, in your very young age,
Maintain all relations, act like an experienced sage,
For it is in each other that we encounter 'Him',
Everyone is important, relationships don't trim.

6

God Guards His Children

Your child is not your slave,
He is not meant to pander to your need,
Your motives are very wrong,
That is why to him you don't heed.

Your child belongs to the Lord,
He for him has planned a mission,
Give him freedom to carry it on,
Otherwise you'll find there will be fission.

Be careful how you treat your child,
For God will be very strict,
Out-pouring of his wrath you'll see,
If he finds that you've had your child tricked.

Don't mess around with God above,
For his children he does guard,
To their aid he'll come with speed,
To defend yourself, you'll have no card.

7

The Children's Play

I watched the children on the shore,
As they asked their mother to play a little more,
On the sands, different designs they made,
Little knowing that soon the waves would raid.

With glee and frolic they did build and draw,
Showing their mother what they did with awe,
Their excited and joyful faces were worth the wait,
Even though the evening was getting dark and late.

When it was finally time to depart,
They walked away with a heavy heart,
On the sand their works did remain,
And in time the waters washed it plain.

Our lives I see are just the same,
For on the sand we're playing a game,
On it our imprints and impression we do make,
And with us we can never them take.

When new energetic and vivacious waves build up,
They'll come with their roar and upturn the cup,
What exists in the end turns to dust,
For new beginnings to take root that's a must.

Then did the kid's play have any meaning,
After the destruction of their work and gleaning?
May not have been worth in the end,
But the joy they derived they did extend.

The children's play outlined life and its circles,
That birth and death the globe encircles,
Only here, it was a matter of little time,
In reality many years pass to make life sublime.

8

Raiding Fear
ೂ೧ ೂ೧ ೂ೧

Fright! Oh, it has me gripped!
My mind and body it has ripped,
I am what you call terror-stricken,
Panic makes my heart beat quicken.

I am suffering from much fear,
Thoughts of attack linger near,
I have my own self to protect,
The danger ahead I do detect.

When things around me do me scare,
My soul, my form is nude and bare,
I have no armor, sword nor shield,
Naked I stand on the bloody field.

The land is parched, cracked and hot,
No grass, no trees, no green patch dot,
No drops of water to quench my thirst,
Fear I experience at its worst.

I don't know why I'm afraid,
But fear and terror have begun their raid,
I find myself in its strong clutch,
I'd like to hide in a rabbit's hutch.

My heart is heavy, it begins to throb,
In my ears the beats move and bob,
They darken the recesses of my mind,
Logical thoughts are lost in the grind.

My body has become pale, white and stiff,
My paralyzed self begins to drift,
Cold and sweaty turn my feet and palms,
There is no gentle breeze that calms.

Then with faith's last straw I do groan,
About my pitiable state I do moan,
The Lord reminds me, how precious I am,
Nations he'll give up for me, his fearful lamb.

In a cloud of dust higher he'll lift me,
Thro' erupting volcano and stormy ocean, he'll steer me,
No scratch, no gash, no wound to dress,
My mind he'll free from all stress.

To walk and go in the name of the Lord,
With faith as a shield and the Word as a sword,
The fear in me into thin air rises,
The Lord has set many surprises.

9
Fear: The Ugly Monster

Fear, you ugly monster! You seem to rule my life,
Creeping in the darkness, in my wounds you turn the knife,
A big block you've laid in the middle, making anxiety thrive,
My life you've got a hold on and personal growth you deprive.

I just wish, I could drown you in the deep blue sea,
For big fish to swallow you up before they smile with glee.
Fear, do you know? That's what you constantly do to me,
You force me back into my hive like a wingless bee.

Oh Fear! How I hope you were long lifeless and dead!
That would put my life in good stead,
I'd then be able to walk keeping upright my head,
I wouldn't have to hide like a ragged shoe under the bed.

Fear, you I hate! You've got me in your grip!
My ambitions, dreams and desires you tear and rip,
Shamelessly you threaten that you'll publicly me strip,
And send me on a naked, quivering trip.

10

Hello, Destiny?

Destiny, Oh Destiny, what is it, that you have in store for me?
You rule my life that I can see! Tell me, how am I, to please thee?
At your feet do I have to bow and please thee with my karma?
Or really do I have to influence you, with an inexplicable dharma?

For you are the one that cryptically charts the course of my fate,
Your enigmatic personality keeps unknown the criteria and the date,
People all around me worship you, as horoscopes they seek,
They who dread your mighty power, try to at the future peek.

But I don't fear you Destiny! 'Cause you are a servant of God most high,
You will kneel at his feet and he will direct you from the sky.
Though imperfect may be my life, my karma and my dharma,
I live in the love of God and his mercy is the guiding rod.

11

Oh, Dear! It's the Stress Again

My tremendous stress led to utter distress,
I couldn't in the least, pare my despair,
How was I, to remain calm or de-stress?
I was not able to prevent the roaring flare.
The weight of the burden I couldn't make it less,
I felt, I was in a coma and blank was my stare.

The tall tower of anxiety I could not tear down,
Its load on my head was too heavy a crown,
In this mental agony, all my emotions began to drown,
And my body wore a pale and sickly gown.
My mood was down cast, my response was a frown,
All I could see was a potholed path, muddy, dirty and brown.

A conscious effort I made to the disquietude attenuate,
I surrendered to God and began to meditate,
Besides my level of fitness I did reevaluate,
And through exercise, physical strength I began to cultivate.
The result simply didn't the trepidation palliate,
But calm, equanimous composure it did reinstate.

So if you want to cruise, a balance please strike,
Between the realms of physical fitness and spiritual psych,
Assign equal weightage and then ride life's bike,
Ensure you won't skid, get punctured by a spike.
This is how you will survive every stress,
And surely it'll never cause you distress.

12

The Happiness Hunt

Happiness, it is a state of mind,
Ironically, very difficult to find,
It plays around and does elude,
It puts the inner self in a good mood.

Happiness, it is a present divine,
Shows that God's grace still does shine,
On those who always praise his name,
However tough it is to play the game.

Happiness, it is a heavenly gift,
The inner spirit, it does lift,
In everything to be content,
Even if you pay high rent.

Happiness, it comes from within,
It cannot ever be stolen,
By any external and hopeless odd,
For it is given to you only by God.

A fervent prayer that's how it's got,
Thanks and praise will destroy the rot,
Faith in the Almighty you need to restore,
And of happiness he will give you more.

Section IV

THOUGHTS OF LIFE

1

Vice & Virtue

Vice and virtue, we all have both,
Vice, we always criticize and disregard,
But virtue we praise and always extoll,
Its development, we never ever retard.

So much importance we give to virtue,
At times of it we are proud,
In other instances we may parade it,
That's the danger; it may turn out to be a shroud.

Of our virtue, if we are conceited,
That makes a vice of self-righteousness,
Then nobody will think you're virtuous,
They'll oppose you with forthrightness.

But that's just one side of the virtue story,
For virtue in its extreme form,
Loses its glory and becomes a vice,
Proper balance should be the norm.

Too much of virtue or too little,
Becomes an anathema for one and all,
For excessive virtue or its scarcity,
Will cause you to stumble and finally fall.

Now don't pamper only one virtue,
Expecting it to yield rich dividend and fame,
For only one part of your self will grow,
The stunted part will make you lame.

So develop all virtues on equal footing,
Take time off regularly to introspect,
So the creepy vice does not slip in quietly,
And your life it won't affect.

2

Justice a Necessity

Justice has to be brought about,
And justice we must in our lives see,
The truth has to be given credence,
The victim, we must hear his plea.

Words, they can be severely contorted,
And used to play a mind game,
Thoughts and opinions they can wrongly influence,
And in the end utilized to unjustly frame.

For in the short term the game seems won,
Though bitterness and angst it does create,
Peace it destroys and hatred it breeds,
When a lie is used as the bait.

Love, peace and joy can only sustain,
When justice is brought to the fore,
Right must infinitely outweigh wrong,
And justice should guide the human core.

3

Can't Have It All

Some have this and some have that,
With what you have, you should bat,
Enjoy the game and play with all your might,
In what you have you should delight.

You cannot get all that is in the world,
For everyone in happiness, deserves to be swirled,
You should find joy in your game,
Live life to the fullest, don't make it lame.

Don't be selfish and covet your neighbor's,
'Cause then in your mission you'll struggle and waver,
You won't achieve it and a millstone it will be,
There won't be an outlet to free the 'me'.

So accept graciously, all that you have been given,
Let thanksgiving and praise be on your lips as your livin,
Use it my friend to brighten every day,
Shine like the sun and make new hay.

4

Chaos Unlimited

Life is chaotic; I have absolutely no control,
Everything's a mess; it's like being haunted by a troll,
The troll is the lack of a system proper,
That puts all situations in utter disorder.

Nothing is definite and nothing is clear,
All is unsettled, I can't see the present here,
But in this mad system of disorder I see,
That a specific pattern is followed to the very T.

Values and ethics comprise the system of order,
That is totally absent so we live on the border,
For payments are taken but deliveries are not made,
Many words are spoken but into oblivion they fade.

So there's no one to rely on and no one to trust,
Minute to minute anxiety causes much frust,
We've continuously to adapt, to each moment each day,
That's how chaos is survived but with stress we pay.

5

Transient Living

Everything is moving and nothing is still,
All is transient including your freewill,
It's the choices that you make every minute of the day,
That leads you on and shows you the way.

With all the movement and transition,
There is extreme disorder and collision,
For all matter is in constant motion,
And if the pace quickens there's instant commotion.

It is the values you've imbibed in your early years,
That will guide your decision without any fears,
Tradition will stand firm as a stable factor,
Even if your field is ploughed fast with a tractor.

In days gone by, we saw ploughing that was manual,
The physical process allowed contemplation that was gradual,
But today the furrows are made too deep and quick,
There's no time for adjustment, the clock continues to tick.

That is the reason for the stress in our lives,
We are wounded daily with very sharp knives
Before the wounds heal, new incisions they cause,
There's no time for curing and no time to pause.

If the particles vibrate with increasing intensity,
Human emotion is suppressed, there's no sensitivity,
Soon you'll see an explosion: a big bang, a boom,
That will sweep all that is built with one stroke of a broom.

Slow down one and all, take things in your stride,
So the gaps in time don't become increasingly wide,
Take decisions properly and on God fix your eyes,
And forever to sorrow say your goodbyes.

6

The Crossroads of Creativity

Children are always taught to be obedient,
And many a times that's much to their dismay,
'Cause the self has to diminish with gradient,
Initially tantrums and sulks will be their play.

However when they learn obedience,
They learn to accept authority's rule,
Playfulness and naughtiness they still want to express,
Creativity they use as a handy tool.

For obedience is nothing but a channel,
That ensures wards to societal norms conform,
Or they'll be wild creatures on a panel,
Who will have no ethics, values or behavioral form.

So nurture creativity in the very young,
For you don't want robots moving around,
Just pressing buttons to make the child obey,
You will land in your lap a zombie, a clown.

7

To Cross a Stream

The stream is broad, the stones are sharp,
I can't see them but on fright I harp,
My flesh it will pierce and cut from within,
The thought of the deep gash distracts my win.

But I have to cross that very stream,
As I live my life on an uneven seam,
The old from my life I have to wean,
I trust the stream's waters to wash it clean.

It'll be like a baptism of new life,
That will wash the fear and abolish strife,
To reach the opposite banks of that stream,
Invigorated, revived, fearless and lean.

Then, for my mission I'll be ready,
To carry it out with firm steps that are steady,
I would have gained the required energetic strength,
To cross any stream, walk any length.

8

Heaven and Hell

On earth, there are two places; they are called heaven and hell,
And every traveler will have to visit both; learn to survive them and to gel.
The places depend on events occurring and situations taking place,
But wherever the traveler may find himself, he will need God's grace.

The places get interchanged from time to time,
And to pass through both you'll need a will sublime.
But all will experience them as they comprise life's journey,
And everyone should at all times appoint the Lord their attorney.

Both places are temporary in nature and somewhat transient,
And this makes the character of the visitors resilient.
They keep on moving from present to future and back,
At the most you can prolong one and make its movement slack.

Then try to be good and in heaven live,
And while you are there, don't to others insults give,
For self-righteousness will threaten, to your good deeds overtake,
And your haughty attitude will your foundation shake.

That will lead to black spots on the spotlessly clean,
And slowly from heaven your position you'll wean.
Your journey to hell will become the forced regime,
And sooner than you know it, heaven will be a distant dream.

In hell you will burn, in a fire that's ablaze,
And the heat will cleanse you, the blemish erase.
Just be patient and the suffering stoically endure,
For that sin this is the only cure.

The fire will change you and reverse your path,
You will slowly be moving to heaven without the wrongdoing cart,
Till again you will find yourself in ultimate bliss,
And self-righteousness at your door, again it will hiss.

And so from heaven to hell one continuously goes,
To get cleansed and to forgive all foes.
Then from hell to heaven again the journey does start,
In this way you are made perfect, with a transformed heart.

9

The Margin of Error

When the margin of error is zero,
And the scope of a mistake is nil,
You will have to play like a hero,
And rightly square up the bill.

When there are no options to back you,
And in all other avenues you find a block,
There will be only one choice in your queue,
That will permit you to create reserve stock.

The risk you can take will then be negligible,
As the benefits are far too little to want,
You will lose more than what is eligible,
And you won't have any treasures to flaunt.

The stress in these situations will be immense,
As backtracking won't be part of the game,
But the experience that you get will be so intense,
And to gain wisdom should be your aim.

10

In Adversity's Face

To laugh in the face of adversity,
Requires inner strength and serenity,
It comes from thorough acceptance,
Of life and its circumstance.

For you know that what has happened has happened,
And let not your spirit be dampened,
But from it learn knowledge and attitude,
Let it build you up with fortitude.

For if someone has wronged you then divine justice is yours,
Although sheer justice can never heal flaws,
But at least you've got it and you're the victor,
You'll have to counsel self and redirect the vector.

If you feel you have an error made,
Realize that there was no option to you shade,
You did what you did to the best you could,
You took on adversity and tall you stood.

11

The Mode of Survival

We have to adapt to imperfection,
And make it suit our need,
For life can never be perfection,
Our minds and attitudes we have to knead.

Knead yourself to fit the groove,
Get yourself exercise and massage,
Adapt soon and make the move,
Or you will be washed out in a lavage.

Survival requires much more than fitness,
Whether it is the body, soul or mind,
See that you trim every inch of fatness,
Become lean to your place find.

12

Black and White vs Wrong and Right

Have you ever tried to classify black and white?
And a clear demarcation between them sight?
For as you move from black right across to white,
You'll find shades of grey depending on the amount of light.

So have you tried to classify wrong from right,
And a clear demarcation between them sight?
For in between you'll find a large area of grey,
And whether it is wrong or right it's difficult to say.

Black and white is as stark as wrong and right,
And a clear demarcation between them is difficult to sight.
Sometimes one may not be able to take a hard stance;
As often imperfections rule circumstance.

It is the result of a freewill, given to one and all,
As each one for conduct has to take a call.
If that call has adverse repercussions,
It will throw all affected into the grey area of discussions.

Then one will have to creatively redesign,
The rules that guided every original sign,
And incorporate between the stark right and wrong,
An area that is grey but still right and strong.

13

Death in Sinking Sands

I stood on the wet sand in just one place,
I thought I'd stand still and at the scenery I'd gaze,
But I found my feet just sinking within,
As the sand covered them, they were hidden.

If I had to continue to stand and not move at all,
Into the wet sand my body would fall,
My inaction would have buried me alive,
And the passivity in me would prevent me drive.

Thus complacency does not lead to mere stagnation,
But it is a process of slow death that is my observation.
So mere self-satisfaction does not ensure your current position,
But it will make you slide back till you fall with delusion.

So move and move and in one place don't sit,
'Cause in a manner tacit you'll find that death has hit.
Even if you want to in one place stand,
Ensure that some water over your feet does land.

As the waves move the sand, it'll wash away,
And in your burial time there'll be a delay,
For movement makes sure that energy moves on,
It gives life to all at sunset and dawn.

14

The Wave of Pride

The ocean, it is large and vast,
With many a tiny, glistening, lilting wave,
Tilting, flitting onwards they move,
The elements of the earth they brave.

From amongst them one was chosen,
Providence had designed a plan and a will,
For it to zoom from height to height,
And frame policy from the highest hill.

That wave, it was just excellent,
No mistake could Providence ever make,
It had brains, brawn and every required skill,
Its inborn talents were far from fake.

Its duty was conscientiously performed,
As it labored, traveled far and wide,
To highest authority it gave account,
Its mission completed from every side.

Soon that wave became aware,
Of its high value and its worth,
Pride and arrogance filled itself,
On lesser mortals, it looked down with mirth.

But that wave never ever realized,
That nature had its chartered course,
And from esteemed height and glory,
It would eventually be pulled down with force.

Right enough, as one day it traveled,
It saw from the top a hard, rocky rock,
If it hit the end was near,
It would be swallowed up by the boiling crock.

But Providence proved to be kind and merciful,
To make amends, gave it time,
For it to establish peace and calm,
So Heaven could welcome it with chime.

At last that wave hit soft sand,
And it did turn to frothy foam,
Its particles spread on the beach,
They returned to Mother Nature's home.

Its repentant soul was very light,
And it reached for the angel's outstretched palms,
Eternally there it will ever be,
It'll sing God's praises and holy psalms.

15

The Essence of Spirituality

Spirituality goes beyond all religion,
It is above gender, caste and creed,
Spirituality is definitely not fiction,
In reality it does thrive and breed.

Spirituality includes all people,
It is universal in nature and in form,
It draws humanity into one circle,
And it unites all with the same uniform.

To attain a level of spiritual oneness,
To basic religion one needs to conform,
To religious laws and tenets one must adhere,
It is daily prayers and rituals that will reform.

So whatever our differences, let it in no way be,
A hindrance to value and respect all humanity.
Happiness and well-being for humankind must be,
And the only criteria should be unity.

16

The Stubborn Flowers

Some drooping flowers that were chosen,
To adorn the altar of God most high,
Felt so wanted and so very full,
To that prized position, they couldn't say bye.

It was there that they had lived their whole life,
Serving God with all their might,
And now the time had come to abdicate,
Get ready to board another, different flight.

Stubborn were they, they refused to vacate,
And wouldn't allow the next to succeed,
For it was that seat that made them great,
Insecurity and anxiety in them began to breed.

They couldn't carry on the required mission,
Of it; they made a messy mess,
And only pain could cause the fission,
Between the seat and them with stress.

It would've been better to elegantly step down,
Instead of bringing upon themselves disgrace,
Grace must abide to give them grace,
And allow fresh flowers to take their place.

17

The Time Accountant

My time on earth is very precious,
To God I need to give account,
Of every passing minute I am conscious,
I must not squander it nor flout.

Useless thoughts and fantasies,
Many have passed thru' my mind,
Taken me to wild exotic ecstasies,
It's been an unreal and fruitless wind.

Thru' this maze, actuality calls,
With its truthfulness and its splendor,
To seek God's visage thru' rise and fall,
To his holy will, myself, I render.

I want to seek his glowing face,
To know his thoughts divine,
I'll fight every battle, run every race,
For thru' my life his glory will shine.

Direct me Lord, please lead and guide,
My time is running out to waste,
From me, your plan, do not hide,
Come to my side with haste.

18

An Untraveled Path

From out of the blue, I was provoked,
To travel a path very much unknown,
And with confusion my mind was choked,
But the desire to walk a less trodden path was sown.

I listened carefully to the voice of intuition,
As a heavy weight on my heart it laid,
And daily from above I received divine tuition,
To carry out his plan many blessings I was paid.

As I walked on the road like a reel it unwound,
And the strips I had to trod became clearer,
With faith and trust, doubt could not abound,
To holiness my steps drew nearer.

19

My Mission Carried Out

I've done my work; I've carried it out,
I've not shirked that is without doubt,
In this my prayer, please notice my pout,
That neither root nor shoot has grown anywhere about.

It was thoroughly useless all that I did,
So much risk I took, my ego I hid,
Much of my time, myself, my stakes I bid,
Was your voice a hoax? Were you just trying to kid?

I'm so sure of you and what you speak,
I know that in our communication there is no leak.
Then what in me do I have to checkmate?
So that your given task I can effectuate.

I praise you Lord for all the hurt in me,
Help me retreat, give me signs to see,
Give me the grace to bend my knee,
Finding joy and making sorrow wee.

20

The Eulogy of the Rejected Soul

I speak for the soul that has no loving acceptance,
I speak for the soul for whom no one spares a care,
To the world that soul is non-existent,
For its earthly journey, it pays a high fare.

The soul that is lonely, the soul that's cast away,
The soul that has no place to go, nowhere to stay,
It is a tragedy that alone it has to move and roam,
To find a suitable, loving and accepting home.

But God hears its prayer and its agonizing groan,
And knows that it may be lost forever.
This irreversible loss, heaven will always moan,
And hence unity with it, it won't sever.

POETIC WORDSCAPES

He'll send his angels from very high,
Who will come to that soul's rescue,
They will nurse it and console its cry,
Well-being in it, they'll renew........

21

The Limit? What's That?

The finiteness of man to the infiniteness of God,
The limitedness of man to the limitlessness of God,
The restrictedness of man to the unrestrictedness of God,
Is what makes us fall flat, prostrate before the Lord.

Our thoughts are few and very few they are,
Our wisdom is limited to not very far.
Our thinking mind is governed by our sensual senses,
It cannot move beyond the human fences.

For we react or respond to what we see or hear,
Our feelings evolve from stimuli, which are close and near,
What we do and what we say are restricted to the world we live in,
But sometimes, we need to transcend the human clamor and din.

To heed right instinct and shun the wrong,
Requires fine tuning of life's fork with its prong,
It's only then you'll be able to surpass the human 'I',
Be united with God and look in his eye.

Our limitedness will then gain a new perception,
And encountering the Infinite will not be a deception,
Then together with God you can live life anew,
And of limitlessness you'll see a different hue.

22

Karma and Dharma

Does karma and dharma really matter?
When one can live in the love of God?
Does goodness really make a difference?
When one lives life by mercy's rod?

My karma is to be good to all,
And its face is compassion, kindness and patience,
It embodies every known virtue,
Whether it's honesty, self-control and obedience.

My karma mainly affects others,
All those around me bear its consequence,
With their curses I'll be smothered,
If I don't live in proper sequence.

POETIC WORDSCAPES

My dharma mainly concerns myself,
And its face is niyam, tapasya, satya and charity.
Its aim is to bring tranquility of mind,
And it uses forgiveness, non-violence and austerity.

But both karma and dharma lead to the highest ideal,
That is to love one and all,
And if you live in the love of God,
You'll have no choice but to take that call.

So know Gods' love and live in it,
And from that will emanate the two,
Automatically you'll find yourself practicing them,
Peace and joy will be your due.

Section V

MELANGE

1

Oneness with Nature

There was no wind, not even a breeze,
That could bring coolness and the hotness ease.
The trees stood still and so did every plant,
The leaves didn't move, they casually said, "We shan't!"
So nature seemed still and nothing did move,
Only a garden sprinkler did water and groove.
The cawing and chirping of the crow and the bird,
Were the only sounds that could be heard.
Two old ladies were taking their regular walk,
Both were silent and not a word did they talk.
The stillness of nature in the morning sun,
Brought tranquil to my mind and with it I felt one.

2

The Stock Market in Verse

The stock market is soaring,
The bulls and bears roaring,
The prices of shares rise and zoom,
The man on the street, his heart goes boom.

The index is reaching heights that are dizzy,
The minds of investors are in a tizzy,
The catch words are 'make fast money',
Everyone wants to accumulate honey.

Is that what the market gives all of you?
A proper investment strategy is overdue.
Time frame, portfolio and risk profile,
One needs to study and go that extra mile.

Can the index be a monetary dictator?
Or is it the only economic indicator?
If it is then, skewed is analysis,
The financial state needs dialysis.

The rising market tells nothing about,
Whether the economy is fat or stout.
The market is driven by demand and supply,
Fear and greed they engulf and belie.

Human emotions swing out of control,
The rational mind is suppressed by the soul.
The frenzy - all investors are in its grip,
Be careful or you may fall and trip.

The capital market, it is an economic tractor,
Though it is governed by more than one factor,
It ploughs, it furrows, and it sows the seed,
But along with that it may breed weed.

It cannot ensure a golden harvest,
Though investors think it is the fastest.
Tips they shoot from the hip,
The grapevine may be the cause of the slip.

Many are mistaken and too much do they trust,
Soon they find their lifesavings turn to dust,
When suddenly the market weakens and crashes,
Despair and distraught across them splashes.

The buying euphoria begins to cease,
Panic-stricken selling begins to tease,
From up to down, the index does spiral,
Market investments are put through a trial.

The bulls and bears stage a massive fight,
The retail investor, what is his plight?
Caught in the midst of a wild battle,
For his dreams, it sounds the death rattle.

For some to gain, others must lose,
Trickery and rumors should not be the ruse,
Whoever decides to play the game,
Mistakes they must not repeat again.

3

The Aroma of Cooking

Cooking is my passion,
It does me entice,
I consider it no ration,
Whether it is spaghetti or rice.

Whatever be the ingredient,
I like to turn and toss,
The flame, the smoke seems so radiant,
The effort is no loss.

To blend, to mix and to match,
Each underlying flavor,
The spice, the taste one must catch,
The food one must savor.

When others eat my steamy food,
And do relish with delight,
They elevate my existing mood,
It makes me feel so bright.

4

The Flowers Tell...

The flowers, they looked pretty,
The flowers, they looked good,
The flowers, they were so beautiful,
As in their vases, they brightly stood.
Color they brought to the dull place,
Uplifted the ambience, decked it with lace.
Intricately woven with fibers so natural,
They were so real and esoterically factual,
The leaves around did enhance their splendor,
Flamboyance they exuberated, joy they did tender.

5

Operation Bug Evacuation

Errands I did by riding in a public car,
The distance it carried me was not far,
Little did I know that my mood would turn sour,
For a tiny bug hid in my clothes that very hour.

Innocently I came home and sat on my bed,
I positioned well a pillow to rest my head,
The bug had now found his cozy warm home,
It crept from my body onto the soft foam.

As I slept peacefully, it on my blood fed,
And multiplied in numbers, I saw with much dread,
In line they crawled and in crevices they crept,
To see them all around many tears I wept.

Helpless I was as I did stare and look,
There was no way to get them out, not even by fluke,
So professional help I sought and for bug treatment I signed,
But with its implementation, the order at home got non-aligned.

Every drape was sprayed and every bed was upturned,
No sofa left out, no cushion was spurned,
Things in storage were just plucked out,
They lay strewn on the floor and all about.

For an hour I shut the house that was so very messed,
I couldn't understand why I was cursed, not blessed,
Into the washing machine went every bit of cloth,
I began to settle the floor and cleanse the rot.

What frightened me was that the exercise had to repeat,
After three weeks the guys would again the bugs beat,
At this time I felt my family's love and support,
As this genus brought me agony, on me, they did dote.

Operation Bug Evacuation is what they performed,
It increased togetherness and to love they conformed,
They helped me through it and gave me every aid,
And to the parasitic bugs good bye I bade.

6

A Lover's Fate

A lover sat canoodling under a tree,
His lass was well positioned on his knee,
On top of the hill they sat, oblivious,
Engrossed in each other, of none they were suspicious.

The hill was secluded and covered with green,
Though in the city it was camouflaged and very serene,
Rocks and bramble made the climb up very hard,
No one would adventure as from snakes had to guard.

So let's come back to the boy and the girl,
While kissing each other they hit a knurl,
This happened to be a beehive just above,
The bees came buzzing, engulfed the two in love.

Astounded, the two had to that moment stop,
Their romantic maneuvers abruptly did flop,
They had to run for cover right down the hill,
With swarms of bees chasing them, to kill.

Gasping, the two to the main street they came,
When the lad took a breath and glanced at his dame,
The bees had fled, from the smoke filled city,
With disheveled hair they looked at themselves with pity.

It was then that Miss-Lass suddenly became aware,
That she had left her handbag right up on the stair,
The lad felt obliged, he had to it get,
He forgot the bees and to climb he got set.

He ran up the hill with quickening pace,
Grabbed the purse and down he did race,
The bees got excited to smell him all over again,
So they attacked him with vigor, inflicting much pain.

He came down the hill with swollen ears and nose,
A dismal state he was in, not a charming pose,
Miss- Lass snatched the bag, didn't care about his head,
That was the last as they were never to wed.

7

The Poor Lad

The young lad had no home to live,
He lived right upon the street,
Odd jobs he found here and there,
To himself support, enjoy a treat.

He worked so hard and earned money more,
That was just above his daily need,
He used some of it and saved the rest,
So on a rainy day it could buy him a feed.

The savings he had no place to keep,
No house, no home nor wooden door,
So a few hundreds in a polythene bag he wrapped,
He hid it on the street above the floor.

Between the poles and the roof, there in a corner indiscreet,
He hid the bundle away from human eye;
The vault: was a public bus stand on the street,
It would never be robbed, no one would even try.

The lad continued his daily work, his chores,
But wrongly he had thought and envisaged,
For birds with their vision, around the bus stop lurked,
They saw the bundle that was camouflaged.

They pecked at it with all their might,
Till bits of plastic descended to the ground,
The bag was torn, the money, it fell from height,
The poor boy's savings were scattered around!

That evening as he came back to his vault,
To take a long look and live satisfied,
He saw no bundle! Was it a foolish fault?
The tortured soul sat on the path and cried.

8

The Battle of the Bulge

A battle she continuously fights, is one of the bulge.
Her soldiers have her failed,
Or have they her treacherously betrayed?
'Cause to soothe the flesh, she did indulge.
So she summoned them, one by one,
To see who was not responsible,
Or even worse, didn't want to be accountable.
She inquired why she hasn't won?
Self Control couldn't grip her with its power,
As shamefully her weakness over it did tower.
Discipline, it couldn't make her its slave,
That is why her will lost out from being brave.
Motivation was enthusiastic about its schedule,
But midway through ran out of fuel.
Eating Healthy was the slogan she did put out,
But it has tripped and turned the scale about.

Exercise & Exercise was the mantra of each new day,
But it was lazy to stretch its legs and play.
Diet & Go Dietary, recipes it had to modify,
But it served wrong meals and could not rectify.
Determination tottered and did go lame,
It could not stand firm and the weight tame.
Fitness it was to be the goal and ideal,
But it failed miserably to strike a holistic deal.
The Mind, it had no peace to be calm and tranquil,
Overeating it did when it felt sentimental.
Therefore she berated their lack of consistent behavior,
As they gave in to desire and the moment to savor.
The supervisory soldier, she nicknamed Drudgery,
She was the General and in her army she didn't want shortcuts or forgery.

9

An Adventure

On an adventure I went to the wild,
The conditions there were far from mild,
In a portable tent of canvas I slept,
All my belongings, valuables in the open I kept.

The cold wind, yes, it gnawed at my chest,
From nature's elements I had no rest,
To swim and raft in the deep river,
Down my spine, it sent an electric shiver.

Crossing a rope bridge in mid-air,
At my nerves and mind it began to tear.
To climb hard rocks and go on mountain hikes,
To my physical self they were like spikes.

To take aim and to air-rifle shoot,
Left me staring, dumb and mute.
Rapelling from the mountain cliff,
Saw me standing shaken and stiff.

A deep satisfaction and fulfillment I got,
By undertaking all in the challenge pot,
As the sticks of the bonfire were set ablaze,
It shielded me from chill, darkness and my mind's maze.

10

The Pristine Peak

To the mountains we decided to go,
The snowcapped peaks they were the glow,
They lured us to their very base,
To climb the cliffs we quickened our pace.

The foot hills they were lush and green,
The air over there was fresh and clean,
We thought peace we'll attain and divinity we'll greet,
When we made our way through the mountain's feet.

Something within gave us a push and a call,
It seduced us but we were afraid we might fall,
With courage to encounter dangers seen and unseen,
We risked our lives like a reckless teen.

As we went higher the greenery ceased,
The mud-colored earth our senses teased,
Occasionally we saw shrubs of sticks and heath,
We looked down from the top and saw the world beneath.

The air became cooler and the terrain barren and rough,
The mountain stood bare, the climb became tough,
Landslides we experienced as loose earth did crumble,
With every step we felt the ground beneath rumble.

But we couldn't stop, we suffered from the mountaineer's craze,
At the pristine peak with awe we did gaze,
As we reached higher, she seductively did entice,
Her brown body she showed through the white lace of snow and ice.

At a certain altitude our woolens we wore,
With caps, boots and mufflers we were covered from head to toe.
The atmosphere was misty, it was like we floated in a cloud,
Fog nipped at our nares our visibility was wound.

The pure, white peak was now not an illusion,
But between it and us there could never be a fusion,
For our extremities turned blue with the air rarefied,
The conditions were harsh, our beings mystified.

We couldn't stay there longer, we would have met our end,
So after caressing the bride's train, we turned the bend.
Snowflakes engulfed us and hypoxia set in,
Headaches and nausea from it we were sufferin'

That's how the peak maintains its distinctive nature,
'Cause to all who come, she acts like a stranger.
After moments of ecstasy they have to go away,
And on the top of the mountain they can never stay.

11

The Rocket Experience

I sat in a simulator, a mock rocket it was,
I strapped myself up, I took a brief pause,
The seat aligned itself parallel to the earth below,
The journey ahead was to be superfast, not slow.

I held tightly onto the handle as the rocket took off,
At the thunderous ignition, I could not even scoff,
It was like a huge bomb that under me exploded,
For a moment my mind was confounded and overloaded.

As I left the launching pad, thrust into the plume of cloud,
Liquids of hydrogen and oxygen flowed out to blend aloud,
Boom! Bang! Boom! Bang! Perpendicular into the air it did propel.
I felt it was my life's end, I heard the death knell.

I imagined the fire between me and the ground,
Thru' acceleration, I gained momentum to exceed the speed of sound,
The burning fuel was such an impetus, a driving force,
With increasing velocity my voice trembled, turned hoarse.

Fortunately the emanating smoke in my nostrils, I couldn't smell,
Though the intensifying vibrations on my being they did dwell,
The speed aided the noise to make the rocket reverberatory,
A newness I experienced that to me was revelatory.

My jaws they were chattering, my teeth they were rattling,
Besides the bones in my body, my joints they were crackling,
I experienced firsthand Newton's Laws of Motion,
Even though the initial feeling was one of commotion.

As the fuel burnt the empty containers were discarded,
And the mass of the rocket gradually retarded,
Over the atmosphere and into orbit we slid,
I viewed the stars and celestial bodies, just like a kid.

Into deep sleep mode we sailed in space,
I felt weightless as I gazed at peace in the face,
I wished, I was an astronaut, when my lips broke into smiles,
Then I'd navigate the cosmos' nautical miles.

12

A Ride in the sea

Over the waves and into the sea,
Our oil-powered boat zoomed like a bee.
The buzzing engine overpowered the high water-wall,
As we went over with a bump we did fall.

The sea was not calm and the waters were fierce,
But our little boat through it did pierce.
Up and down, the ride was very bumpy,
As the waves made patterns that were very lumpy.

Over high crescent and into low trough,
Our little boat found the ride rough.
As water was sprayed right into our face,
The nano droplets on our lips, shone like glace.

The salt in the mist made our eyes burn,
And with nothing to hold on to we couldn't even turn.
Squinting, we tried our best to enjoy the visual effect.
With the leaping of dolphins the scene was perfect.

Our ride back posed no challenges,
As the natural waves prodded the boat on like phalanges.
The high wall of water this time, brought us safely to beach,
We were filled with gladness to it reach.

13

Adjust your Sail

Once I sat in a sail boat, on an excursion I went,
To the middle of the sea where an edifice stood;
The air it was still, the waters they were calm,
Over the lilting waves, lilted my boat of wood.

The boat had a mast: tall, straight and upright,
Attached to it was a sail which elegantly fluttered,
The blowing wind, suddenly, its direction reversed,
Flustering our boat which nervously shuddered.

The sailors on board were nonchalant,
One balanced himself on the edge of the deck,
Lying on air, parallel to the water, he maneuvered the sheet,
Until the wind aided the boat, to turn its neck.

So in many instances in life my friend,
The direction of the wind cannot be changed,
Just adjust your sail to turn the bend,
And you won't be confronted with a situation so deranged.

14

Storm to Calm

My life, it was so stormy,
I couldn't understand why?
It was so dark and scary,
In loneliness my prayer was a sigh.

My small boat how it tossed,
In undulating waves so high,
Sea sickness ruled and me it bossed,
To make me writhe in pain, weep and cry.

That crisis it had me shaken,
At my foundation with its deep root,
Why am I despised, forsaken?
Where are you Lord, are you a brute?

"Certainly not", was the answer,
Though it came many years late,
"It was only the early sign of disaster,
I wanted to save you and change your fate."

"From the rough and roaring sea I led you,
To the still, gentle, lilting of the quieter water,
For the rest of the journey in peace to pursue,
Your steps to guard and prevent you falter."

15

The Adventurous Artist

O Lord, you are an artist,
You create with utmost originality,
Sketching for you is timeless,
For your drawings are in totality.

In them there is nothing amiss,
For all is proportionate,
Without a reference point to draw,
Is your genius quotient.

Each scene is so picturesque,
All the colors contrast or blend,
Every technique is so unique,
Onlookers, on a twirl they send.

And if with some stroke you're displeased,
On it you tactfully paint to reset,
Bringing forth what is called evolution,
So the final picture one never can get.

When do you intend to stop?
For minute flaws still you see,
That the perfect you're perfecting,
For what? I fail to see!

Why are you beautifying this landscape?
For a million years you're painting,
In which exhibition, do you propose to unveil it?
On that my mind is straining.

16

To the Ends of the Earth

I did not ask for anything,
And yet you gave me all!
I am not worthy of anything,
'Cause often I do fall.

You took me to a wondrous place,
To show me all of your creation,
The beauty I saw on the earth's face,
Surpassed all my imagination.

The penguins, the seals and the whales,
To view in their own surrounding,
Were sights that in my mind prevailed
My senses they kept on hounding.

The misty mountain, the stony height,
As barricades tall they stood,
Protecting flora and fauna with all their might,
They did the best they could!

The turbulent waters, the roaring sea,
Boiled hard upon the rocks,
Their white, foamy froth I could see,
At my inner being Mr. Adrenaline knocks.

Your artistic strokes, you did complete,
As you blended the rainbow's colors.
The different shades did flit and fleet,
Amazement resounded in my hollers!

The waves they danced, to and fro,
Each one was clothed in a shade of blue,
Reflecting the sun and the sky they did glow,
My gaze on them was stuck with glue.

The salty smell, the touch cold and hot,
Stimulated my nerves beneath,
The air I drank from the ocean's pot,
It invigorated my spirit's seat.

The vineyards, the forest and every tree,
Split into a spectrum of green,
The leaves shone and glistened with utmost glee,
They were a breathtaking scene.

POETIC WORDSCAPES

The earth's jewels were an array of flowers,
Ecstatically they smiled at me,
Elegance and joy were sprayed like showers,
To smell and touch, I bent my knee.

Each picture was so unique,
How did you get each idea?
My experience with nature's boutique,
Was an all-encompassing panacea.

Oh! Thank you Lord, for all you've made,
For humanity to admire and enjoy,
Help us to keep it in top grade,
So gen-next can also experience joy!

17

All Good Things are Free

I heard the twittering of the birds,
The fluttering of their wings,
I saw them soar up in the sky,
And dive into the water rings.

Their voices echoed in the air around,
Enchanted all the earth,
Their weightless bodies flitted up and down,
I take for granted all their worth.

Colorful and elegant were their clothes,
The flowers on their stalks did sway,
From side to side, to and fro,
Their broad smiles brightened up the day.

The insects, the animals and the bees,
Lolled upon the grass so green,
Enjoying all without paying any fees,
The whole world had a glossy sheen.

God did care for all of these,
Gave them food and clothes,
Provided shelter and a gentle breeze,
Washed and wiped away their woes.

When I look back on my life,
I see how much, God for me cares,
He's shielded me from each sharp knife,
He's never asked me to pay the fares.

About the Author

Ranjana Rebelo Monteiro lives with her husband and two teenage daughters in the city of Mumbai. Being her birthplace she has experienced its cosmopolitan culture to the fullest and the blessedness of its people. Besides, her travels both in India and abroad have influenced and broadened the horizon of her mind to view all situations and events from a wider perspective.

Qualified as a MMS (Master's in Management Studies) from the University of Mumbai, Ranjana began her career as an Equity Research Analyst with one of the city's reputed stock brokers. From there she moved to working with an asset management company.

Ranjana's commitment in caring for her children launched her into a new creative trajectory which has seen her move in its locus ever since. With two instruments in hand the paint brush and the pen, Ranjana is an artist who paints landscapes and a poet who writes wordscapes. To add to the creative passion, she is also a culinary expert who specializes in cakes and bakes. Besides teaching she is also involved in social activities.

www.ingramcontent.com/pod-product-compliance
Lightning Source LLC
Chambersburg PA
CBHW031348040426
42444CB00005B/229